Amasis, an Egyptian Princess: A Comic Opera in 2 Acts

Philip Michael Faraday

"AMĀSIS"

AN EGYPTIAN PRINCESS

A COMIC OPERA
IN TWO ACTS

WRITTEN BY

FREDERICK FENN

COMPOSED BY

PHILIP MICHAEL FARADAY.

VOCAL SCORE 6/- NET

METZLER & C⁰ LIMITED
40 TO 43, GREAT MARLBOROUGH STREET,
LONDON. W.

RUTH VINCENT

H.M.S. PINAFORE;

OR.

THE LASS THAT LOVED A SAILOR,

An entirely Original Nautical Comic Opera

WRITTEN BY

W. S. GILBERT

COMPOSED BY

ARTHUR SULLIVAN.

Vocal Score, complete ... ... 4s. net; or, bound in cloth, gilt, net	7	6
Pianoforte Score, complete ... ... net	4	0

List of Songs, &c.,
PUBLISHED SEPARATELY FROM THE ABOVE.

"He is an Englishman." (Song and Chorus)	4	0
"Sorry her lot who loves too well." (Josephine's Song)	4	0
"Fair moon, to thee I sing." (Song) Captain Corcoran	4	0
"I am the Ruler of the Queen's Navee!" (Song and Chorus.) Sir J. Porter ...	4	0
"I am the Captain of the Pinafore." (Song and Chorus.) Captain Corcoran ...	4	0
"Never mind the why and where-fore." (Trio) Josephine, Captain Corcoran, and Sir J. Porter ...	4	0
"Little Buttercup." (Song.) Mrs. Cripps	4	0

Arrangements.

H.M.S. Pinafore Selection for the Pianoforte ... ... Charles Coote, Jun.	4	0
H.M.S. Pinafore for Violin Solo ... ... Montgomery, net	1	0
H.M.S. Pinafore Fantasia for the Pianoforte ... ... By Edouard Dorn	4	0
H.M.S. Pinafore as a Duet for the Pianoforte ... ... By Edouard Dorn	5	0
H.M.S. Pinafore Selection of Airs. Arranged for the American Organ ... By J. M. Cowan	4	0
H.M.S. Pinafore for Violin and Pianoforte ... ... By Henry Parker	4	0
"Little Buttercup" Arranged for the Pianoforte ... ... By Michael Watson	3	0
Ditto Arranged as a Duet ... ... By Michael Watson	3	0

Dance Music
ARRANGED BY
CHARLES GODFREY
(Bandmaster, Royal Horse Guards).

H.M.S. Pinafore Quadrille (Solo or Duet) ... ... Charles Godfrey	4	0
H.M.S. Pinafore Waltz (Solo or Duet) ... ... Charles Godfrey	4	0
H.M.S. Pinafore Galop (Solo or Duet) ... ... Charles Godfrey	4	0
H.M.S. Pinafore Polka ... ... Charles Godfrey	4	0
H.M.S. Pinafore Lancers (Solo or Duet) ... ... Charles Coote, Jun.	4	0
H.M.S. Pinafore Singing Quadrille ... ... J. Pridham	4	0

ORCHESTRAL PARTS OF THE DANCE MUSIC.
Small Orchestra, 1s. 4d. net. Full Orchestra, 2s. net.
H.M.S. Pinafore Selection, for Septet Band, arranged by Charles Coote, 1s. 4d. net.

Metzler & Co., Ltd., Great Marlborough St., London. W.

PRODVCED AT NEW THEATRE, Aug. 9ᵀᴴ. 1906.

BY

Mʀ LOUIS CALVERT.

"AMĀSIS"

AN EGYPTIAN PRINCESS

A COMIC OPERA IN 2 ACTS

WRITTEN BY

FREDERICK FENN

COMPOSED BY

PHILIP MICHAEL FARADAY.

METZLER & Cº, LIMITED,
40 TO 43, GREAT MARLBOROUGH STREET,
LONDON, W.

VOCAL SCORE 6/- NET
Dº BOUND 8/6 ,,
PIANO SCORE 3/6 ,,
BOOK OF WORDS 1/- ,,

TELEGRAMS:–
"LERMETZ, LONDON".

		25 copies	50	100	250	500	1000
VOCAL SCORE	CODE	394	02394	05394	06394	08394	09394
PIANO SCORE	CODE	25 copies 410	02410	05410	06410	08410	09410

"AMĀSIS"

An Egyptian Princess.

A COMIC OPERA IN TWO ACTS.

Written by FREDERICK FENN.   Composed by PHILIP MICHAEL FARADAY.

Amāsis IX	...	...	..	(Pharaoh of Egypt) ...	Mr. RUTLAND BARRINGTON
Prince Anhotep	...	...	... ...	...	Mr. ROLAND CUNNINGHAM
Cheiro	...	...	...	(a Scribe) ...	Mr. WHITWORTH MITTON
Nebenchari	...	...	...	(a High Priest) ...	Mr. NORMAN SALMOND
Ptolemy Theopompus Allakama	...	(Court Embalmer) ...			Mr. HERBERT ROSS
Sebak	...	...	(Keeper of the Crocodiles)		Mr. LAURI DE FRECE
Psamtik	...	...	...	(Captain of the Guard)	Mr. FRANK PERFITT
Zopyrus	...	...	...	(A Wine Merchant)	Mr. G. MACKARNESS
Town Crier	...	...	... ...		Mr. LEONARD CALVERT
Second High Priest	...	...	... ...	...	Mr. F. AUBREY MILLWARD
First Expert Witness	...	...	... ...	...	Mr. B. FRASER
Second „ „	...	...	... ...	...	Mr. J. CLULOW
Third „ „	...	...	... ...	...	Mr. C. GREGORY
Fourth „ „	...	...	... ..	...	Mr. W. DERWENT
Natis	...	...	..	(A Maid) ...	Miss MADGE VINCENT
Anna	...	.	(in attendance on the Princess) ...		Miss EMMIE SANTER
Qeresa	...	...	(Fanbearer to Pharaoh) ...		Miss M. STATHER
Atossa	...	...		...	Miss MARION MARLER
Ladice	...	...		...	Miss EVELYN BERESFORD
Kleis	...	...	Wives of Merchants of Memphis	...	Miss ETHEL GRAHAME
Tachot	...	...		...	Miss GLADYS ERSKINE
Ranofre	...	...		...	Miss KATHLEEN McKAY
Rhodopis	...	...		...	Miss MAX HINTON
Nitetis	...	...		...	Miss PAULA St. CLAIR
Kassa	...	...		...	Miss POPPET McNALLY

AND

Princess Amāsis ...	...	(Daughter of Pharaoh)...	Miss RUTH VINCENT

Mummy Guards—Messrs. Skinner, Stedman, Wingfield, Brodie, D'Anville, Marsland.

Priests—Messrs. Johnson, Hoscroft, Bennett, Birts.

Citizens—Misses Birkbeck, Reeves, Macey, West, Dunbar, Hodges, Morrison, Gardner, Wentworth, Maynard, Moore.

Messrs. Digues, Brook, Ferguson, Harberd, Wingrove, Swinhoe, Ashley, Walshe, Hopwood.

ACT I. - Courtyard of the Palace of King Amāsis at Memphis.

ACT II. - Another View of the Courtyard of the Palace.

"AMĀSIS."

AN EGYPTIAN OPERA IN TWO ACTS.

CONTENTS.

AMĀSIS

AN EGYPTIAN PRINCESS

A Comic Opera in Two Acts.

WRITTEN BY
FREDERICK FENN.

COMPOSED BY
PHILIP MICHAEL FARADAY

OVERTURE.

M.8393.

Nº 1.— OPENING CHORUS.

Copyright, U.S.A., and Austria-Hungary. 1906, by Philip Michael Faraday.

Ring, oh, ring a wed‿ding peal, ___ Pharaoh's daughter comes to wed, ___

Ring, oh, ring a wed‿ding peal, ___ Pharaoh's daughter comes to wed, ___

Ring, oh, ring a wed‿ding peal, ___ Pha‿raoh's daughter comes to wed, ___

Ring, oh, ring a wed‿ding peal, ___ Pha‿raoh's daughter comes to wed, ___

Stamp the deed with roy‿al seal, _____ Shower blessings on her head.

Stamp the deed with roy‿al seal, _____ Show‿er blessings on her head.

Stamp the deed with roy‿al seal, _____ Show‿er blessings on her head.

Stamp the deed with roy‿al seal, _____ Show‿er blessings on her head.

M.8898.

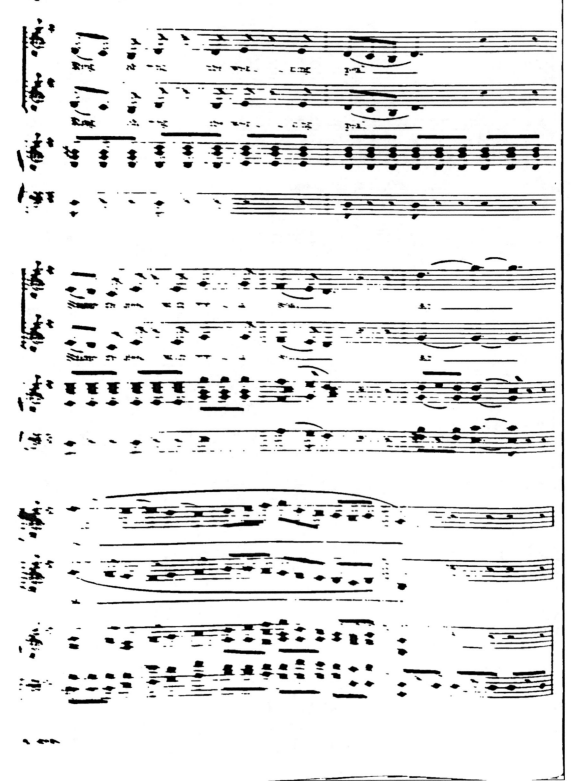

12

Ring, oh, ring the wed _ ding peal, _____

Ring, oh, ring the wed _ ding peal, _____

Stamp the deed with roy _ al seal, _____ Ah! _____

Stamp the deed with roy _ al seal, _____ Ah! _____

Ah! _____

Ah! _____

M. 8898.

MALE CHORUS.

Tenor.

Hi - ther comes a Prince of Phi - læ, Brav - est of a king - ly race, ___ Not a des - ert foe - man wi - ly Dares to meet him face to face, ___ Not a des - ert foe - man

Bass.

Hi - ther comes a Prince of Phi - læ, Brav - est of a king - ly race, ___ Not a des - ert foe - man wi - ly Dares to meet him face to face, ___ Not a des - ert foe - man

seal, _____ Shower bless _ ings on her head!

seal, _____ Shower bless _ ings on her head!

seal, _____ Show _ er bless _ ings on her head!

seal, _____ Show _ er bless _ ings on her head!

Ring, oh, ring a wed _ ding peal Ring, oh, ring a wed _ ding

Ring, oh, ring a wed _ ding peal Ring, oh, ring a wed _ ding

Ring _____ Ring, oh, ring, oh ring a wed _ ding

Ring, oh, ring a wed _ ding peal Ring, oh, ring a wed _ ding

peal, Stamp the deed with roy _ al seal, Stamp the

peal, Stamp the deed with roy _ al seal, Stamp the

peal, Ring _____ Stamp the

peal, Stamp the deed with roy _ al seal Stamp the

deed with roy _ al seal.

deed with roy _ al seal.

·deed, the deed with roy _ al seal.

deed with roy _ al seal.

Nᵒ 2.—DUET. "Wont you marry me."

(NATIS and SEBAK.)

1. I start_ _ _ed in life as a poor lit_tle maid, To
2. If you're a Princess all the world comes to woo, To

wait on the love_ _ly A_ma_ _sis; But I
hang on a word or a smile; Though A_

M.8393.

Copyright. U.S.A., and Austria-Hungary 1906, by Philip Michael Faraday.

don't like the work and it isn't well paid, Oh how try _ ing a wait _ ing maid's
_ ma _ sis is pret _ ty, well, I'm pret _ ty too— It's on _ ly a dif _ fer _ ent

place is! . I must think of my _ self and not sit on the shelf, I can't
style. Tho' I've giv _ en up hope, I would love to e _ lope If e _

be in ser _ vice for ev _ _ _ er; But what can you do if they
_ lope:ments were on _ _ ly in vogue; _____ And I know if some scamp made me

don't come to woo Whenyou're shy and are not ve _ ry cle _ _ ver? I'm
with him de _ camp. I should fall down and wor _ ship the rogue! Long a _

Dance.

Nọ 3.– SOLO. "My name is Ptolemy."

(PTOLEMY.)

Copyright, U.S.A., and Austria - Hungary. 1906, by Philip Michael Faraday.

mighty Pharaoh's Court Embalmer, Inventor of the Mummy. You
whole of his wealth must come to me As the profit on my trading. This
bring your enemies to me For the National grand museum. If
income tax has never paid— Each passive bad resister— Who

possibly think my trade abhorrent Or fancy I charge you
quid pro quo for my honest toil Each poor defunct a
you've a friend who's in the way Don't ever try to
irritates our crocodiles Each Company di

highly, But here, if you please, is my Royal Warrant To
grees on, And I make immortal the mortal coil Of
harm him, But a handsome cheque to me you pay, And I
rector— Who chivies sacred cats with tiles, Each

deal with each Cor _ pus Vi _ _ le. I've a dif _ fer _ ent style for the
thou _ sands ev _ ry sea _ _ son. Oh, my bus _ i _ ness grows in a
quiet _ _ ly em _ balm him. You real _ _ ly nev _ er
naugh _ ty vi _ vi _ sec _ tor. By migh _ _ ty Phar _ aoh's

high and low. To the rab _ ble I'm Pto _ le _ my Sons and Co. But the
way sur _ prising, Tho' I spend not a far _ thing on ad _ ver _ tising, And the
need to fret Be _ _ cause you're in old I _ saacs debt; You
wise de _ cree No vi _ cious rogue em _ balmed may be, You're

high _ toned a _ ris _ too _ ra _ cy Deal with Pto _ le _ my, Lim _ i _ ted,
ver _ iest boo _ by thus must see That em _ balm _ ing's a ve _ ry soft
mere _ ly say the chap has died, Then gloat up _ on him
mere _ ly tres _ pass _ ing on my time If per _ chance you've commit _ _ ed

Fils et Cie, Go to a-ny mu-se-um and there you may see 'em They've
job for me. The whole of E-gypt saves, you see. For
mum-mi-fied. Oh, it swells the pro-fits, fa-mous-lee. Of
orimin-al crime, No an-ar-chist need come to me— To

1st, 2nd & 3rd Verses. | Last time.

all of them been em-balmed by me. Fils et Cie.
Pto-le-my, Lim-i-ted, Fils et Cie.
Pto-le-my, Lim-i-ted. Fils et Cie.
Pto-le-my, Lim-i-ted,

V.S. for DANCE.

M.8898.

Dance.

Allegro moderato.

Nº 4. SOLO. "I prayed for life."

CHEIRO.

VOICE.

PIANO.

Moderato.

I pray'd for life, a lit-tle life, and now— Come death! There is no life for me. Ah, me!— Ah, me! Be-fore the Gods I bow. Ah, me!

In two grey eyes I saw my light and sun. Go, sun! Go, sun! There is no sun for me Ah, me! Ah, me! The si_lent night has won. Ah,_ me!

cresc. molto e agitato.

Here, where I look'd on love, I come to lie, Nor grieve, nor grieve. Two eyes were dim, two eyes were dim for me Ah, me! Ah, me! The Gods are kind to me, The Gods are kind, I die.

Nº 5. SOLO. "Little Princess, look up!"

(AMASIS.)

1. Last night the moon beamed on me and cried Little Princess, look up! Do you know why I shine with a radiance fine Little Prin-
2. The beautiful sun in the golden east cried Little Princess, look up! To love is beholden my radiance golden Little Prin-

_cess___ look up! Oh my love is the sun the
_cess___ look, up! On my la _ dy the moon is

great Sky King, And we love with a love un _ wa _ ver _ ing, Sweet
mirrored my light, We are King of the day and Queen of the night, Sweet

Queen of the earth be hap _ py as I Laugh for the
Queen of the earth in your mai _ den pride Let your lov _ er

_ en _ tan _ do.   a tempo

Prince your sun is nigh! } Laugh__ and look up!
meet a ra _ diant bride! }

34

Ah! Ah! Ah! Ah! Ah! Ah! Ah! Ah! Ah!

Presto

ff

M. 8898.

Nº 6. DUET. "Tell me you hate all other men."

(AMASIS and ANHOTEP.)

-hap-py ev-er af-ter, af-ter, af-ter, Un-hap-py ev-er af-ter.

Dance.

ff

p

p staccato.

ff

ffz

ANHOTEP.

came a quick ces_sa_tion of the row. For though
_flect_ed on her ve_ry sor_ry state She
fish_pond then I put that cat to bed And as

Tab_by's lives are le_gion If you smash the dor_sal re_gion They have
should have had nine lives at least But though I cut off one poor beast, I
I'm an ear_ly ris_er Why, then no one is the wis_er Ex_cept

1. & 2. *rall.*
scarce_ly time to gasp out one Mia _ _ ow!
could_n't well in_sure the o_ther eight

colla voce.

3.
pus_sy, and poor pus_sy, well she's

dead!

p

NO. 8. ENTRANCE and CHORUS. "King Pharaoh's Guard."

Tempo di Marcia.

PIANO.

CHORUS OF GUARDS. BASSES.

We are King Pharaoh's Guard. Cus_to_dians of his Cats; We dust the Sphinx and Py_ _ramids, And brush the Roy_al hats.

M.8898.

Copyright, U.S.A., and Austria-Hungary. 1906, by Philip Michael Faraday.

TENORS.

We are King Pharaoh's Guard; We guard his king _ ly hon _ our. If

he re _ quires a Roy _ al wife We choose a Pri _ ma Don _ na.

We choose a Pri _ ma Don _ na.

ff

We are King Pharaoh's Guard For bet‿ter or for worse; We

pp

We are King Pharaoh's Guard For bet‿ter or for worse; We

fol‿low him where‿e'er he goes, And keep his pri‿vy purse. And

fol‿low him where‿e'er he goes, And keep his pri‿vy purse. And

ff

ff

all who do our will of‿fend They find their pros‿pects

all who do our will of‿fend They find their pros‿pects

ff

marred   It's   all   ve_ry well   to   be   a King   But it's

marred   It's   all   ve_ry well   to   be   a King   But it's

bet_ter   to   be   his   Guard.

bet_ter   to   be   his   Guard.

ff

Nº 9. SONG and CHORUS. "Once Egypt was a dreary land."

(PHARAOH.)

VOICE.

PIANO.

Allegretto.

1. Once E - gypt was a drear - y land, ruled by a drear - y King, An op - er - a - tic
2. But the eve - ning of the bat - tle, said my gal - lant men to me "To - mor - row, oh, our
3. So one and all drew me a - side, and mur - mur'd soft and low, We're go - ing back to
4. They found my pre - de - cess - or in the count - ing - house a - lone, And as he would - n't

M 8393.

Cap-tain I, who made the wel-kin ring! So to a de-sert
Cap-tian, we shall dead as mut-ton be! For the foe-men far out-
E-gypt, and we will not strike a blow! It's a ve-ry sim-ple
ab-di-cate they knifed him to the bone! And the pop-u-lace cried

reg-ion With a most un-ru-ly le-gion I was
-weigh us, And most cer-tain-ly will slay us, And
thing To re-move the pre-sent King; For,
"Vi-va!" When they heard he'd died of fev-er. Then they

sent to quell some A-rabs, and their wick-ed necks to
what's the good of dead-ness to the likes of such as
though he may not ab-di-cate, I think we'd make him
said to me, "Oh, Cap-tain, what's the mat-ter with the

Nº 10. SEPTETTE. "Seven poor ladies"

Tempo di Gavotte.

PIANO.

1st WIFE.

Seven poor la _ dies of Mem_phis are we,___ Con_demned to this grave in_

_dig _ ni _ ty___ By each lord and mas _ ter. Fear_ing dis_as _ter De_

M. 8898.

50

hook or by crook You must not real_ly~ You must not look.

PHARAOH.
Come here a min _ ute and lis _ ten to me,___ I've a sug_ges _ tion that

good may be:___ Ask two or three Young fel _ lows to tea, And

I'll keep an eye On the lot you see. I fan _ cy the humour would

soon be - gin If you shut them out as they shut you in, And

later your quarrel you'll e - ven up With just a few drops in each

WIVES.

hus - band's cup. We thank you immense - ly for this ad - vice To

pay out our hus - bands would be so nice. We'll do what you say by hook

M. 8893.

№ 11. DUET. "Your Majesty!"

ANHOTEP and PHARAOH.

M.8393.

PHARAOH.

price _ less gift, her path shall be all ro _ ses. I

ANHOTEP.
Your Ma _ jes_ty!

know that's what, I know that's what each im _ be_cile sup _ po_ses. your

PHARAOH.

Ma _ jes_ty! my love has made me bold! Youth's fol _ ly makes, youth's

ANHOTEP.

fol _ _ ly makes me thank the gods I'm old.___ And

58

if it please your Ma_jes_ty I fain would wed in

PHARAOH.

haste. I'd have you know her mo_ther, boy, is for_ty round the

ANHOTEP.

waist. Your Ma_jes_ty! your Ma_jes_ty! you may re_tain her

mf

PHARAOH.

mo_ther. I on_ly mean, I on_ly mean she'll grow just such an_

staccato.

M.8393.

Nº 12. CHORUS. "Sign the Contract."

Copyright, U.S.A., and Austria-Hungary. 1906, by Philip Michael Faraday.

Each re-la-tion Tear is shed-ding. Troth now plight-ed, All ex-ci-ted,
Sun shine glor-ious This her dow-ry. All is readiness, Soon be headiness

Each re-la-tion Tear is shed-ding. Troth now plight-ed All ex-ci-ted,
Sun shine glor-ious This her dow-ry. All is readi-ness, Soon be headi-ness

Each re-la-tion Tear is shed-ding. Troth now plight-ed All ex-ci-ted,
Sun shine glor-ious This her dow-ry. All is readi-ness, Soon be headi-ness

Each re-la-tion Tear is shed-ding. Troth now plight-ed All ex-ci-ted,
Sun shine glor-ious This her dow-ry. All is readi-ness, Soon be headi-ness

Quite de-light-ed, Ac-qui-es-cing. Bridegroom fear-less Bride so peer-less,
Some un steadiness When all's o-ver. High hopes veri-fied, Bridegroom merrified,

Quite de-light-ed, Ac qui es-cing. Bridegroom fear-less Bride so peer-less,
Some un steadi-ness When all's o-ver. High hopes veri-fied, Bridegroom merrified,

Quite de-light-ed, Ac qui es-cing. Bridegroom fear-less Bride so peer-less,
Some un-steadi-ness When all's o-ver. High hopes veri-fied, Bridegroom merrified,

Quite de-light-ed, Ac qui es-cing. Bridegroom fear-less Bride so peer-less,
Some un-steadi-ness When all's o-ver. High hopes veri-fied, Bridegroom merrified,

Nº 13. SONG. "I'm adviser to this Royal pair."

SEBAK and CHORUS.

Allegro moderato.

1. I'm ad _ vi _ ser to this Roy _ _ al
2. It's quite a roy _ al re _ si _ dence from
3. My ar _ chi _ tect has done his best to
4. It's a most suc _ cess _ ful blend _ ing of the

pair, Tra la la la la, Tra la la la la! I'm the
ev'ry point of view, Tra la la la la, Tra la la la la! And
tin _ ker up the Sphinx, Tra la la la la, Tra la la la la! The
modern and antique, Tra la la la la, Tra la la la la! The

CHORUS

on _ ly fel _ low liv _ ing they could trust/with this af _ fair, Tra la
when I've re _ up _ hol_stered it, 'twill be as good as new, Tra la
ser _ vants have their quar_ters in the basement with the sinks, Tra la
sort of place where lov _ ers like to spend a hap _ py week, Tra la

SEBAK.

la la la, Tra la la la la! They
la la la, Tra la la la la! I've en _
la la la, Tra la la la la! I
la la la, Tra la la la la! And

want _ ed an es _ tab _ lish_ment not like sur _ bur _ ban vil _ las, All la _
_ gaged a staff of ser _ vants and a girl to do the char _ ing, While the
an _ a _ lysed the sub - soil to make sure that it was sand _ y, While
though my in _ no _ va _ tions may of _ fend the ul _ tra pur _ ists, I've

M.8898.

_bur_nums and a sum_mer-house o'er - run with cat - er - pil - lars, But a
lifts and all the light-ing is con - tract-ed for by War - ing, The
when the Prince is late at night he'll find the tram_way hand - y; I
put a rail - ing round it to keep off ob - tru - sive tour-ists, The

man - sion large e - nough for two, and pos - si - bly a kid, So I
fur - ni - ture's all Chip-pen-dale made by a man called Mos - es, And the
thought un - de - cor - a - ted stone was just a shade pro - sa - ic, So I've
weak - est point a - bout it is the lack of ven - ti - la - tion, Still,

hired from the a - gents a most room - y py - ra - mid.
Art and Craf - ty bed-steads will be far from beds of ro - ses.
had Sir Will - iam Rich-mond down to dab it with mo - sa - ic.
as a mod - ern re - si - dence, it's quite a rev - e - la - tion.

M.8898.

CHORUS.

1. 2. & 3.

So he hired from the a-gents a most room-y py-ra-mid.
And the Art and Craf-ty bedsteads will be far from beds of ro-ses. D.C.
So he had Sir Will-iam Richmond down to dab it with mo-sa-ic.

So he hired from the a-gents a most room-y py-ra-mid.
And the Art and Craf-ty bedsteads will be far from beds of ro-ses.
So he had Sir Will-iam Richmond down to dab it with mo-sa-ic.

So he hired from the a-gents a most room-y py-ra-mid.
And the Art and Craf-ty bedsteads will be far from beds of ro-ses. D.C.
So he had Sir Will-iam Richmond down to dab it with mo-sa-ic.

So he hired from the a-gents a most room-y py-ra-mid.
And the Art and Craf-ty bedsteads will be far from beds of ro-ses.
So he had Sir Will-iam Richmond down to dab it with mo-sa-ic.

1. 2. & 3.

D.C.

CHORUS.

4.

Still, as a modern re-sidence, it's quite a rev-e-la-tion.

Still, as a modern re-sidence, it's quite a rev-e-la-tion.

Still, as a modern re-sidence, it's quite a rev-e-la-tion.

Still, as a modern re-sidence, it's quite a rev-e-la-tion.

4.

ff

Nº 14.—FINALE ACT I.

Allegro moderato.

PIANO.

NEBENCHARI. (Spoken.)

Dogs and scum and roystering vermin, Bow before the Royal ermine

Because of this distressing rumour— The King is in a vicious humour. His

Majesty has left his meal; The royal soup is getting cold; No

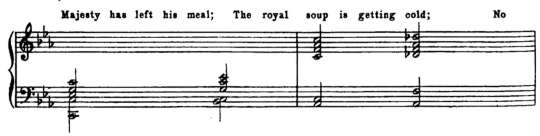

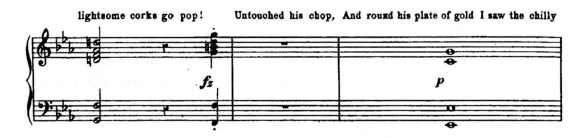

lightsome corks go pop!   Untouched his chop, And round his plate of gold I saw the chilly

fat congeal.   Cringe!   Bend   each   knee's   obsequious

hinge: For   he   has   sworn   he   never   more   will   dine

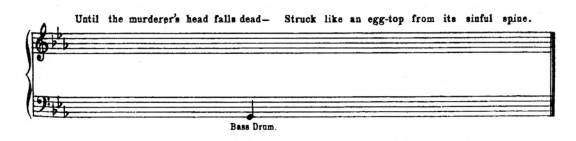

Until   the   murderer's   head   falls dead—   Struck   like   an   egg-top   from   its   sinful   spine.

Bass Drum.

M.8893.

a_ny_one's kill'd her it's tit for tat Whether no_ble or low caste cur. Has

a_ny_one's kill'd her it's tit for tat Whether no_ble or low caste cur. Has

a_ny_bo_dy seen our cat? Pus_sy, pus_sy, puss, puss, purr! The

a_ny_bo_dy seen our cat? Pus_sy, pus_sy, puss, puss, purr! The

on_ly clue is that where she sat We found these fragments. of fur!

on_ly clue is that where she sat We found these fragments of fur!

vil_lain who did it shall sure_ly hang, Or be stood on his head in a butt of mo_lass_es.

Shroud this wanton re_vel_ry, Wave the crinkled crape; Who-ev_er did this de_vil_ry

Ne_ver shall es_cape. Sound the funer_al drum— Pre_pare a roy_al tomb, It

CHORUS.

Sound the funer_al drum— Pre_pare a roy_al tomb, It

Timp:

is decreed This bloody deed Shall shroud the world in gloom. Take heed, The mourner's weed Assume;

is decreed This bloody deed Shall shroud the world in gloom. Take heed, The mourner's weed Assume;

Till the murderer we unearth We will not suffer love or marriage, Be-trothal, death, nor birth.

Till the murderer we unearth We will not suffer love or marriage, Be-trothal, death, nor birth.

2nd PRIEST.

If you this e-dict do dis-par-age, In-dulge in re-vel-ry or mirth— In

kisses, twins Or of her sins;We foretell some grave miscarriage,Of the justice of the King,

Lento.

CHORUS.

Much un_call'd for suf_fer_ing.

Much un_call'd for suf_fer_ing.

3rd PRIEST.

Re_concile your hearts to woe, Dis_perse and

Lento.

go Nor smile,and sing We would not have un_call'd for suf_fer_ing.

CHORUS.

You wretched masses And

You wretched masses And

NEBENCHARI.

PTOLEMY.

Who is this vicious knave, by thun_der? Ah! I

won_der If it will break a roy_al heart And

sore up_set the ap_ple_cart? But see yon youth whose

strong right arm em_bra_ces The willowy waist of the

most fair Am_a_sis, His ash_en looks por_

tray Blood spilt And guilt; I deep-ly grieve this is his

AMASIS.

wed-ding day! Oh,

CHORUS.

Sop.

Alto. We deep-ly grieve this is his wed-ding day!

Tenor.

Bass. We deep-ly grieve this is his wed-ding day!

p

PTOLEMY.

hold your peace, old man; I beg you, go a-way. I fear, Your Po-ten-cy this

pp

gives the show a-way. To think that he should go and stow a-way Poor Pussy.

rall.

NEBENCHARI. *Recit,*

Tell me, how, sir, We con-des-cend to ask you ci-vil-ly; Have you con-nived at a-ny way pri-vi-ly The death of a Roy-al mous-er?

ANHOTEP.

A—las! great priest, 'tis true she is a gon—er, Quite thought-less-ly I dropp'd a brick up—on her; By all the laws of

p leggiero.

eyes to light love's flame, Rash fool to play this thought _ less

game, This thought _ less game, Your life was not _ your own, Be -

This thought _ less game,

_ cause of your fol _ ly She's all me _ lan _ cho _ ly, She must live out her life all a _

_ lone. _ A _ lone! And ev _ en your death won't a _ tone! A _ tone! She must live out her

A _ lóne! A _ tone!

life all a _ lone. If I'd had your chances Of winning her glances .I

would have risk'd nothing, I own_ I own. I would have risk'd nothing, I own. 'Tis a

I own.

sor_ry e _clipse With your name on her lips; She must

CHORUS. A sor_ry e _clipse With your name on her

A sor_ry e _clipse With your name on her

M.8393.

live out her life all a _ lone;   I would have done better, I   own.

lips.

lips.

Recit.   PTOLEMY.

Of this   terrible sin this has   quite con _

AMASIS.

_vinced her.   But   that won't prevent me dy_ing a   spins_ter.   Oh! weigh one Cat, though

val_ua_ble and rare   A _ gainst   my life_long   a _ go _ nised des_pair,

NEBENCHARI.
Suit_a_ble princes Grow thick as leaves in Vallamba_ro_sa. A_way with him! **GUARDS.** We go, sir.

NEBENCHARI. *ad lib.*
He must be tortured now he's caught; And send to me a full re__port.

PSAMTIK.
We'll place the dog in a dún_geon deep, And cross__ex_am_ine him closely, We'll ex_tract from him a whimsic_al tale If we sti_mu_late him jo_cosely. We'll note how'neath our tor_ture's grim He'll

M.8393.

sup - pli - cate and grovel, Our re - port will be as a - mus - ing as A

modern sensa - tion - al novel.

CHORUS.

We'll place the dog in a dun - geon deep And

We'll place the dog in a dun - geon deep And

cross - ex - amine him closely We'll ex - tract from him a whim - si - cal tale If we

cross - ex - amine him closely We'll ex - tract from him a whim - si - cal tale If we

stim - u - late him jo - cosely. We'll note how 'neath our tor - tures grim He'll

stim - u - late him jo - cosely. We'll note how 'neath our tor - tures grim He'll

sup - pli - cate and grovel, Our re - port will be as a - mus - ing as A

sup - pli - cate and grovel, Our re - port will be as a - mus - ing as A

AMASIS. (In strict time.)

Be kind, be kind to

mod - ern sen - sa - tion - al no - vel.

mod - ern sen - sa - tion - al no - vel.

him, I know your gen - - er -

- os - i - ty, The sit - - u - a - tion

slower.

p

If in the dim for-got-ten past you ev-er had a mo-ther, Who

poco accel. *a tempo*

heard you lisp your Al-pha-bet and made you kiss each o-ther, By

rallentando. *Recit.*

her grey hairs I beg of you to treat him like a brother. I'm ve-ry young, I

do not know. per-haps you had no mo-ther. These things to me are all a

mys-te-ry; I ne-ver stud-ied Natural His-to-ry, But

I will be your sis_ter if you'll treat him like a bro_ther. This

This

weak_ness we must smo_ther. No, we ne_ver had a mo_ther, And our

weak_ness we must smo_ther. No, we ne_ver had a mo_ther, And our

Pa_ter was a ha_ter of all sen_ti_ment or weep_ing, We'll not

Pa_ter was a ha_ter of all sen_ti_ment or_weep_ing, We'll not

N.8893.

die beneath assault and bat_ter_y, In halt_ing verse My dy_ing

curse Shall spifflicate your Sacred Catter_y.

Allegro agitato.

ff

I curse their fur; It shall drop off in patch_es; I curse their claws; They'll poison

fp tremolo.   fp

scratches; I curse their tempers, They'll grow like Di _ ogenes; I curse their

wooing And their little progenies; I curse their brains; They'll get con-

_ges _ tion; I curse their food; They'll have in _ di _ ges _ tion. I curse their home life, I curse their morals; Their eyes shall be scratch'd Out in frequent quarrels. I curse each whisker, I curse each tail; They shall sing out of tune, Their voices fail. I curse their liv _ ing and to hu _ mour all these pop _ u _ lar fal _ la _ cies It is my curse, that each shall die nine deaths from pa _ _ ra _ ly _ sis.

M.8393.

98

M.8898.

yet the terrors of the night shall pale Before the pos-si-bi-li-

-ties of day, 'Till, when the sun is heaven high at noon,

Recit. *ad lib.*

Death he will welcome as a Roy-al boon. For not till the sun has mounted to the crown of heaven's proud

dome, Shall my mounting wrath be ap-peased and my eag-er heads-man strike

marcato.

home.

Strike him! Lynch him!

Strike him! Lynch him!

Death and fu - ry, Lynch our judge and lynch our ju - ry.

Death and fu - ry, Lynch our judge and lynch our ju - ry.

Stone him to death. Put him to death!

Stone him to death. Put him to death

102

Put him to death Strike him! lynch him! Strike him! lynch him!

Put him to death Strike him! lynch him! Strike him! lynch him!

Put him to death _____ to death.

Put him to death _____ to death.

ff

M.8393.

End of Act I.

ACT II.

№ 15.- OPENING CHORUS. "Arma Virumque Cano."

(NEBENCHARI and PRIESTS)

Lento.

PIANO

(NEBENCHARI)

Ar_ma virum_que ca_no, Quod erat demon_strandum. Ah!____ Ve_ni, vidi,

(CHORUS.) (NEBENCHARI)

vi_ci, Status quo ante bellum. Ah!____ Pri_mus in_ter pares,

(CHORUS.) (NEBENCHARI)

Quod erat faci_endum. Sic transit gloria mundi, Re_ducti_o ad ab_surdum. Ah!____

CHORUS.

M.8898.

№ **16.**—SOLO and CHORUS. "These Cats plague my life."

(NEBENCHARI and CHORUS)

M.8893.

Chorus.

warders. But they have to be kept from mauruaders, For
na_tion. Oh, it adds to the great com_pli_ca_tion Of a
dox_y. But still we are fear_ful_ly fox_y, We

But they have to be kept from mau_rau ders, For
Oh, it adds to the great com pli_ca_tion Of a
But still we are fear_ful_ly fox_y, We

such are the High Priest_ly or_ders. Folk should
High Priest's mag _ni_fi_cent sta_tion When his
rule all the coun_try by prox_y; What we

such are the High Priest_ly or_ders. Folk should
High Priest's mag ni_fi_cent sta_tion When his
rule all the coun_try by prox_y; What we

take more pre_cau_tion, When death is their por_tion To keep
sym_pa_thies lie With poor peo_ple who die Just be
do on the sly We can al_ways de_ny If in

take more pre_cau_tion, When death is their por_tion To keep
sym_pa_thies lie With poor peo_ple who die Just be
do on the sly We can al_ways de_ny If in

out of the way, To keep out of the way, To keep
cause we're a Cat, Just be cause we're a Cat, Just be_
pub_lic we be, If in pub_lic we be, If in

out of the way, To keep out of the way, To keep
cause we're a Cat, Just be cause we're a Cat, Just be_
pub_lic we be, If in pub_lic we be, If in

1st & 2nd.　　　　　Last time.

out of the way of their warders.
_cause we're a Cat_rid_den_na_tion.
pub_lic we be or_tho_ _dox_y.

out of the way of their warders.
_cause we're a Cat_rid_den_na_tion.
pub_lic we be or_tho_ _dox_y.

Dance.

Nº 17.—SOLO. "The morning's heartless Sun."

(AMASIS)

1. The morn- ing's heart- less
2. The stars which watched us

sun will gild The roofs of this ___ proud
plight our troth, We trust ___ ed to ___ their

M.8898.

ci - ty;   Nor   heed   my   heart   dis -
blind - ness;   Their   steel - y   eyes   de -

mayed   and chilled: Why   won't   the   sun __ show   pi - ty?   The
ny   us   both   The   milk   of   hu - man   kind - ness.   The

moon   to - day   will   flood   a - gain   The   gar - den   of   this
day   dawns   like   an   ope - ning flow'r   Though   my   glad dream   is

Pal - ace;   It   may   be   fool - ish
shat - tered;   I   think   the   world   in

Nº 18.-SOLO. "The Veriest Gambler I."

(CHEIRO)

The ver - iest gam - bler I, Of all who cast the die. The years to - day I stake and play To win my la - dy's eye. The bold - est lo - ser I, Al - though the end be

M. 8393.

Copyright, U.S.A., and Austria - Hungary. 1906, by Philip Michael Faraday.

nigh. A look she bent In won_der_ment, So let it be— I

die. An ea__sy task have I, Not

poco accel

mine to make her sigh, My life would grieve her

Un__de_ceive her, Be_fore I fail—good_bye.

Ped.

Nº 19. DANCE.

Copyright, U.S.A., and Austria - Hungary. 1906 , by Philip Michael Faraday.

№ 20.– SONG. "Lovely Woman."

(PHARAOH)

M.8393.

Copyright, U.S.A., and Austria-Hungary. 1906, by Philip Michael Faraday.

though we fre_quent _ ly are told That beau_ty is a snare, Of
told her if she'd be my bride I'd shield her from all shocks, And
_no_ther rea_son I could see For choos_ing one so fair, That

beau _ ty, quite as much as gold, We like to get our share. But we
she could cast all care a_side And dai_ly darn my socks! But I'm
she and I would tru_ly be A most ro_man_tic pair! But— I

rit.

Tempo di Valse.

find when our beau_ty is won That our trou_ble has on_ly be_gun, We
ra_ther in_clined to ad_mit That al_though she had beau_ty and wit, She was
find there is al_ways the chance That you may have too much of ro_mance, And

Chorus of Ladies.

must not be jeal_ous Or else she may tell us That home to her mother she'll run! We
well o_ver for _ ty, In_clined to be naughty, We should not have suit_ed a bit! But we're
He_len of Troy Though a beau_ti_ful toy is a doll that may lead you a dance! We

cresc.

SOLO.

find when our beau_ty is won That our trou_ble has on _ ly be _ gun, She will
ra ther in_clined to ad_mit That al _ tho' she had beau_ty and wit, Su _ i _
find there is al_ways the chance That you may have too much of ro_mance, Still she

ff   *p*

say if we're hurt At her want_ing to flirt, Do you fan _ cy you've mar_ried a nun? __
_cide with a snake Was a sil_ly mis_take But I don't think she knew that it bit! __
did not con_sent And to Par_is she went But it was'nt the Par_is in France!

1st & 2nd | Last time

My
My

M.8393.

Nº 21. TRIO. "This outbreak was wholly unlooked for!"

(PTOLEMY, SEBAK and ANHOTEP.)

My___ judgement you've tried to dis-place not at all to your taste.

-quali-fy, It is not at all *comme il faut;* He's a dif-fi-cult beggar to

Oh, a ve-ry hard row I must hoe. mol-li-fy;-

120

CHORUS.

M. 8898.

124

M. 8898.

Oh! a de_li_cate ques_tion that

Kings sometimes go to per_di_tion.

It's a lit_tle too late for con_

rai_ses.

_tri_tion, con_tri_tion.

You may both of you tod_dle to blaz_es.

CHORUS.

You may both of you toddle to blaz-es, You may both of you toddle to blazes, It's a

lit_tle too late for con _ tri_tion, contrition, You may both of you toddle to blaz _ es.

Dance.

Nº 22. DUET. "Oh, this world has one oasis."

ANHOTEP and AMASIS.

M.8898.

AMASIS.

I would my wea_ry heart would break, Why are sad hearts so much too

strong? If from my arms my love they take, To

wish to die can_not be wrong. Dear heart, could we but change our

pla_ces, Would you live on with_out Am_a_sis? Oh,

dear~est love, I would that I Were bold to live___ as you to die.

ANHOTEP.

Sweet~heart, look up, and do not shrink Be~fore these ras~cals un~der~bred,

Yet know the bit~ter cup I drink, Is of the tears I've made you

Nº 23.-SOLO. "A lonely little maid."

(NATIS.)

Allegretto.

VOICE.

PIANO.

mp

1. I'm a
2. I'm

lone_ly lit_tle maid, oh, a ve_ry lone_ly maid, Con_
so a_fraid to ask; oh, it's ter_ri_ble to ask; You

_demned to mar_ry ug_ly Ptol_e_my. But I
are so ve_ry beau_ti_ful, and I'm so ve_ry plain. I'm not

Copyright, U.S.A., and Austria-Hungary. 1906, by Philip Michael Faraday.

do not want to wed, I would soon_er far be dead, Oh, he's
good e_nough for you, But what is a girl to do, I may

not at all the kind of chap for me. Still, I
nev_er get a_no_ther chance a_ _gain. I'm not

am a lit_tle shy; oh, yes, ve_ry, ve_ry shy. And the
good e_nough for you, but I'm much too good for him; The

sort of chap that I could love is shy as he could be. Lit_tle
drift of these re_marks you sure_ly now must see. It's a

maid - ens go out walk - ing, But they may not do the talk - ing, And I
ve - ry bold sug - ges - tion, But if you would pop the ques - tion, You could

know that I am most un - maid - en - ly. Do you
save me from that wick - ed Ptol - e - my. Or

rall.

a tempo

know, oh, gal - lant Psam— oh, tru - ly hand - some Psam, You
if you will not speak,— per - haps you dare not speak, Just

lead a ve - ry i - dle self - ish life. Oh,
let me hold your hand and hear the worst. You

M.8898.

Psam _ tic; gal _ lant Psam It's wait _ ing here I am, And you
need _ n't say a word, But just show that you have heard, Oh! I

real _ ly would be bet _ ter if you had a lit _ tle wife!
know its ve _ ry sud _ den, but I've loved you from the first.

Dance. (After 2nd Verse.)

No. 24. QUARTETTE "The Verdict."

(PHARAOH, NEBENCHARI, PTOLEMY and SEBAK.)

M. 8393.

138

But

A

But

Of course he can't be em _ balmed ___

But

But

PHARAOH.

mode of death that's ra_ther fun_ny Is done with ants and a

NEBENCHARI.

pot of hon_ey We've a text book full of un_speak_a_ble tortures With a

PTOLEMY.

spec _ ial chap _ ter de _ signed for Courtiers I've still one com _ fort

M. 8893.

sweet, if small   All of his wealth to   me   will   fall.

Ph.   No.   I   don't see that   at   all.

Neb.   No.

Pt.   Oh!

S.   No.

How.   Much do you think he's   got

How.

How.

How.

M. 8898.

Nº 25. SONG. "The inference is obvious."

PHARAOH and CHORUS.

Moderato.

VOICE.

PIANO.

PHARAOH.

1. That a man should have am _ _ bi _ _ tion will be
Mon _ arch may not spec _ _ u _ late he
told that we shall have to spell in
found it hard to find a rhyme for

rea _ di _ ly ad _ mit _ ted, And there should be in _ tu _
must have cer _ tain cred _ it, And so I formed a
man _ ner more pho _ ne _ tic, And if we want to
"Are we get _ ting Squeam _ ish?" It real _ ly took an

M.8898.

144

M.8893.

slower.

in_ference is ob_vi_ous you see It is just as plain as an_y_thing can
in_ference is ob_vi_ous you see It is just as plain as an_y_thing can
in_ference is ob_vi_ous you see It is just as plain as an_y_thing can
in_ference is ob_vi_ous you see It is just as plain as an_y_thing can

be It's a sovereign to a shil_ling, that a per_son do_ing kill_ing, Will dis_
be For dis _as _ ter you are planning if the stuff that you are canning Is some
be If it must be u _ ni _ ver _ sal it is cer_tain ev _ 'ry nurse'll, Have to
be Does a squeamer go a squeaming as a dreamer goes a dreaming? Can it

CHORUS.

_cov _ er that he can _ not do it free. The in _ ference is ob _ vi _ ous you
an _ i _ mal that laid him down to dee. The in _ ference is ob _ vi _ ous you
teach it in the ba _ bies nur _ ser _ y. The in _ ference is ob _ vi _ ous you
hop a _ bout and bite us like a wasp? The in _ ference is ob _ vi _ ous you

M.8898.

see   It is   just   as plain as an _ y _ thing can   be.   I'm a
see   It is   just   as plain as an _ y _ thing can   be.   Do not
see   It is   just   as plain as an _ y _ thing can   be.   What a
see   It is   just   as plain as an _ y _ thing can   be.   If we

Mon _ arch who   is   will _ ing to   al _ low   a bit   of kill _ ing, But   I
hes _ i _ tate   a min _ ute when you   find   out what   is   in it, Eat   the
chance you will   be miss _ ing, if   you   stop _ to think when kiss _ ing, Must   I
can't ar _ range   to catch   it   we   shall   real _ ly have   to watch it, So   that

1. 2. & 3.

stip _ u _ late they mustn't go   for me.   2. Though a
can and let   the rest of it   go   free.   3. We're
do   it with a *K*   or with a   *C*?   4.   I
if   it does pursue   us   we can

D.C.

4.

flee!

Nº 26.–SOLO. "Long, long ago."

(AMASIS.)

VOICE

PIANO

Moderato.

mf

Long, long a _ go in far off times, A law was made— a

law was made. That a _ ny man led forth to die, Should be reprieved if

there passed by A kind _ ly maid— a kind _ _ ly maid.

M.8898.

You'll
find it in yon dus _ ty tome, I'm ve _ ry sure— I'm ve _ ry sure. The Gods give her this power to save; Her in _ no _ cence may rob the grave If she be pure— if she be pure.

And now, I pray, no childish sin, My soul doth stain—my soul doth stain. Let it be mine, this pow'r of grace, That I may boldly meet his face. Nor weep again— nor

weep a_gain! The kind _ ly Gods who plant each spark Of vi _ tal flame— of vi _ tal flame, Blot out the ter _ ri _ ble of _ fence Be _ _ cause of one maid's in _ no _ cence, His life I claim— his life I claim._

Ped. ❋ Ped. ❋

Nº 27. FINALE.

seal _____ Show-er bless-ings on her head!

seal _____ Show-er bless-ings on her head!

seal _____ Show-er bless-ings on her head!

seal _____ Show-er bless-ings on her head!

Ring, oh, ring a wed-ding peal,   Ring, oh, ring   A wed - ding

Ring, oh, ring a wed-ding peal,   Ring, oh, ring   A wed - ding

Ring, oh, ring a wed-ding peal,   Ring, oh, ring, oh ring,   A wed - ding

Ring, oh, ring a wed-ding peal,   Ring, oh, ring,   A wed - ding

AMASIS.

'Twas giv'n to you a-lone. A gainst harsh death to in ter- vene, So true and brave a friend you've been A friend you've been Your life is not your own. There'd be tears in our gladness If you walk_ed

CHORUS.

SOLO.

M. 8898.

CHORUS.

Tra la la la la! Tra la la la la! Tra la la la la la la la la la!_____

la la la! Tra la la la! Tra la la la la la la!_____

la la la! Tra la la la! Tra la la la la la la!_____

la la la! Tra la la la! Tra la la la la la la!_____

Success of the London Season.

A NEW COMIC OPERA
"AMASIS"

Written by
FREDERICK FENN.

Composed by
PHILIP MICHAEL FARADAY.

Vocal Score	- -	net 6/-
do. (In Cloth)	- -	„ 8/6
Pianoforte Score	-	„ 3/6
Book of Words	-	„ 1/-

SEPARATE NUMBERS 2/- EACH NET.

Lovely Woman, (in G)	Sung by	Mr. Rutland Barrington.
Little Princess, Look up! (in G)	„ „	Miss Ruth Vincent.
The Mornings Heartless Sun, (in E♭)	„ „	Miss Ruth Vincent.
Long, long ago, (in D)	„ „	Miss Ruth Vincent.
The Veriest Gambler I, (in A♭ & C.)	„ „	Mr. Whitworth Mitton.
I Prayed for Life, (in E♭)	„ „	Mr. Whitworth Mitton.

Selection for the Pianoforte, by George Byng   -   **2/- net.**
(Full Orchestra 4/- net. Septett 2/8 net.)

Valse, arranged by Carl Kaps   -   -   -   **2/- „**

Lancers,   „   „ „ „   -   -   -   **2/- „**
(Full Orchestra 2/- net. Septett 1/4 net.)

LONDON:
METZLER & CO., LTD.,
42, GREAT MARLBOROUGH STREET, W.
And of all Music Sellers.

A. C. MACKENZIE'S

New Operetta

ENTITLED

"Knights of the Road."

Libretto and Lyrics by

HENRY A. LYTTON.

Produced at the Palace Theatre.

SONG	"Though Love's a Rose" (Soprano)	2s. 0d. net.
SONG	"The Locket Song" (Tenor)	2s. 0d. „
HUMOROUS SONG	"I'm so nervous" (Baritone)	2s. 0d. „
MADRIGAL	"Ring the Joy Bells" (S.A.T.B.)	0s. 3d. „
	AND	
SONG	"Who'll serve the King?" (Baritone)	2s. 0d. „

COMPLETE VOCAL SCORE with LIBRETTO - - - - 2s. 6d. „
AND STAGE DIRECTIONS

(Fees for Representation of the above may be obtained from the Publishers.)

METZLER & Co., Ltd.,

40 to 43. GREAT MARLBOROUGH STREET. LONDON. W.

METZLER & CO.'S OPERA-BOUFFE SERIES,

Complete with Libretto, Music, Description of Dresses, and Stage Directions.

			s.	d.					s.	d.
†Offenbach	...	"Rose of Auvergne"	1	0	†Boullard	...	"A Fit of the Blues"	...	1	0
†Hervé	...	"Chilpéric"	2	6	†Lecocq	...	"Retained on both sides"	...	1	0
†Offenbach	...	"Forty Winks"	1	0	V. Gabriel	...	"Grass Widows"	...	1	0
†Hamilton Clarke	"The Silver Trout"	...	1	6						

OPERAS ARRANGED FOR THE PIANOFORTE.

			s.	d.				s.	d.
Chilpéric	...	Hervé	2	6	Don Giovanni (all the favourite airs)	Mozart	...	0	6
Anna Bolena (arranged by Devaux)	Donizetti	2	6	Il Barbiere di Siviglia	...	Rossini	...	0	6
La Traviata (arranged by Rimbault)	Verdi	2	6	Der Freischütz	...	Weber	...	0	6
H.M.S. Pinafore	...	Arthur Sullivan	3	0	Carmen. Opera	...	Georges Bizet	0	0
Aladdin the Second	...	Hervé	4	0	Henry VIII. Incidental Music	Arthur Sullivan	3	0
La Reine de Saba	...	Gounod	6	0	Nell Gwynne	...	R. Planquette	3	0
Princess Toto	...	Frederic Clay	3	0			Or bound in cloth, gilt, net	5	0
Our Diva	...	Victor Roger	2	6	Red Hussar	...	Edward Solomon	3	0

OPERAS, CANTATAS, AND INCIDENTAL MUSIC.

A Fishy Case. Operetta for Children. A. J. Caldicott. 2s. 6d.

Aladdin the Second. Vocal Score. By Hervé. Price 5s.

†*Carmen.** By Georges Bizet. Vocal Score complete (English words), 6s.; or handsomely bound in cloth, gilt letters, 9s. 6d. Vocal Score complete (French words), 12s.; or handsomely bound in cloth, gilt letters, 15s. Vocal Score complete (Italian and German words), 12s.; or handsomely bound in cloth, gilt letters, 15s. Pianoforte Score complete, 6s.; or handsomely bound in cloth, gilt letters, 9s. 6d.

The Festival. (Ballad of Haroun al Raschid.) Poem by Archbishop Trench. Set to music for soli, tenor, and bass. Chorus and Orchestra by J. Frederick Bridge, Mus. Doc. Price 1s. net.

Cousin Kate. Operetta. By Meyer Lutz. Price 6s.

†*Dreamland.** Cantata. By A. Matthison and Virginia Gabriel. Price 12s. Separate Numbers and Voice Parts may be had.

†*Evangeline.** Cantata. By Virginia Gabriel. 7s. 6d. Separate Numbers and Voice Parts may be had.

Fanfan la Tulipe. Opéra-Comique en Trois Actes. Musique de L. Varney. French vocal score, 12s. net.

Fleur-de-Lys. Vocal Score. By L. Delibes. Price 6s.

Gelmina. Grand opera. By Rinelli and Prince Poniatowski. Price 21s.

†*Graziella.** Cantata. By Lonsdale and Virginia Gabriel. Price 15s.

†*Harvest Home.** (A Cantata.) By G. B. Allen. Vocal Score complete, 2s. 6d.

†*H.M.S. Pinafore,** by W. S. Gilbert and Arthur Sullivan. Vocal Score complete, 4s.; or handsomely bound in cloth, gilt letters, 8s. Pianoforte Score complete, 2s. 6d.

Henry VIII. Incidental Music composed by Arthur Sullivan. (Containing King Henry's Song, Graceful Dance, Water Music, &c.) Vocal Score complete, 2s.

L'Arlésienne. By Georges Bizet. Suites 1 and 2. Piano Solo, 3s. each net.

Red Hussar. A Comedy Opera in Three Acts. Written by H. P. Stephens, Music by Edward Solomon. Vocal Score, 5s. net; or bound in cloth, 7s. 6d. net.

La Jolie Fille de Perth. Opera by Georges Bizet, Vocal Score complete (French Words), 15s.

†*La Reine de Saba.** Opera by Ch. Gounod. Vocal Score complete (English words), 10s. Pianoforte Score complete, arranged by Georges Bizet, 6s. The celebrated Processional March, 4s.

Lara. Grand Opera. Vocal Score. By Maillart. Price 18s.

L'Arlésienne (Drama in 4 Acts). The Music composed by Georges Bizet. Vocal Score complete (French words), 5s. The celebrated Minuet for Pianoforte Solo, 4s.

The Fishers. A Cantata. Written by Henry Ross. Composed by J. M. Coward. Price 4s. net. Chorus Parts, each 3d.

Le Maître Péronilla. Opera by Offenbach. Vocal Score complete (French words), 15s.

Les Pêcheurs de Perles, by Georges Bizet. Vocal Score complete (French words), 15s.

*Our Diva.** Comic Opera in 3 Acts. By V. Roger. Vocal Score, 4s. net. Piano Solo, 2s. 6d. net.

*Nell Gwynne.** Vocal Score. By H. B. Farnie and R. Planquette. Price 5s. Or bound in cloth, gilt, 7s. 6d. net.

*Princess Toto.** Comic Opera by W. S. Gilbert and Frederic Clay. Vocal Score complete, 6s.

†Robin Hood. (A Cantata.) By John L. Hatton. Vocal Score complete, 2s. 6d.

Our Diva. Comic Opera in Three Acts. Written by P. Ferrier and F. Carré. English Version by C. M. Rae. Music by Victor Roger. Vocal Score, 4s. net.

*Saint Ursula.** (Sacred Cantata.) The Poem (founded on the ancient Legend) by R. E. Francillon. Music by Frederic H. Cowen. Price 4s. net. Handsomely bound in cloth, 6s. net.

Shepherd of Cornouailles. Operetta. By Virginia Gabriel. Price 5s. Separate Numbers may be had.

†The Babes in the Wood. (A Comic Cantata.) The words by Thomas Ingoldsby. Composed by Georges Fox. Vocal Score complete, 2s. 6d.

The Bohemians. Written by H. B. Farnie, and adapted to music by Offenbach. Price 6s.

The Fire King. Dramatic Cantata by Maud Hargreaves. Music by Walter Austin. Price 8s. net. The separate Voice Parts may be had.

*The Sorcerer,** by W. S. Gilbert and Arthur Sullivan. Vocal Score complete, 5s.; or handsomely bound in cloth, gilt letters, 7s. 6d.

†*The Widow of Nain.** A Sacred Cantata. Composed by A. J. Caldicott, Mus. Bac. Cantab. Price, paper covers, 6s. net.; boards, 4s. net. Separate Voice Parts, 6d. each.

Melodies (18). Chant et Piano. (The English words by Theo. Marzials, J. Oxenford, and others.) By A. Goring Thomas. Price 6s. net.

†*Ulysses.** Tragedy in 4 Acts. The Music composed by Ch. Gounod. Vocal Score complete (English words), 7s. 6d.

Who's the Heir? Operetta. By G. March and Virginia Gabriel. Price 5s. Separate Numbers may be had.

Widows Bewitched. Operetta. By Hamilton Aïdé and Virginia Gabriel. Price 5s. Separate Numbers may be had.

Windsor Castle. Opera Burlesque. By F. C. Burnand and F. Musgrave. Price 5s.

† *The Orchestral Parts and Score may be had on application to the Publishers.*

• *Lists of the separate Songs, Pianoforte Arrangements, Dance Music, Arrangements for Violin, Cornet, Flute, Harmonium, &c., post free on application to* METZLER & CO., Ltd. 37, MARLBOROUGH STREET, LONDON, W.

THE SORCERER

AN ORIGINAL MODERN COMIC OPERA

WRITTEN BY   COMPOSED BY

W. S. GILBERT   ARTHUR SULLIVAN.

ARRANGED FOR THE PIANOFORTE BY
BERTHOLD TOURS.

Vocal Score, complete ... ... 3s. net, or bound in cloth, gilt, net 5 0
Pianoforte Score, complete ... ... net 5 0

List of Songs, &c.
PUBLISHED SEPARATELY FROM THE ABOVE.

"When he is here." (Aria) 4 0
"The Vicar's Song." (Ballad.) Dr. Daly 4 0
"Happy young heart." (Aria.) Aline 4 0
"For love alone." (Ballad.) Alexis 4 0
"My name is John Wellington Wells." (Song.) Mr. Wells 4 0
"She will tend him." (Quintet) 4 0
"It is not love." (Ballad.) Alexis 4 0
"Engaged to so-and-so." (Song.) Dr. Daly 4 0

Arrangements.

The Sorcerer. (Fantasia.) For Pianoforte ... ... B. RICHARDS 4 0
" " As a Duet ... ... B. RICHARDS 4 0
The Sorcerer. (Fantasia.) Pianoforte ... ... E. DORN 4 0
The Sorcerer. (Brilliant Fantasia.) Pianoforte ... ... B. F. HARVEY 4 0
"Happy young heart." (Valse Brillante.) Pianoforte ... ... B. F. HARVEY 4 0
"Ring forth, ye bells." (Chorus) ... ... W. SMALLWOOD 4 0
"Oh joy ! Oh joy !" (Chorus) ... ... W. SMALLWOOD 4 0
"Happy young heart." (Aria.) Pianoforte ... ... W. SMALLWOOD 4 0
Selection of Airs. Pianoforte ... ... H. W. GODFREY 4 0
Minuet from the Opera. Pianoforte 1 6
Gavotte from the Opera. Pianoforte ... ... MICHAEL WATSON 3 0
" " " Duet ... ... MICHAEL WATSON 3 0

Dance Music.
Arranged by CHARLES D'ALBERT.

The Sorcerer Lancers. (Solo or Duet) 4 0
The Sorcerer Quadrille. (Solo or Duet) 4 0
The Sorcerer Waltz. (Solo or Duet) 4 0
Orchestral Parts of the above may be had.

INCIDENTAL MUSIC TO SHAKESPEARE'S
HENRY VIII.
COMPOSED BY ARTHUR SULLIVAN.

Complete, Price 3s. net.
Orchestral Score and Parts Published.

Metzler & Co., Ltd., Great Marlborough St., London. W.

"THE HUMANOLA"
LATEST and CHEAPEST
PIANO PLAYER.
MADE IN ENGLAND.

RÖNISCH PIANOFORTES
UPRIGHTS FROM £45
GRANDS FROM £75

MASON AND HAMLIN
ORGANS
LATEST MODELS
THE ALEXANDRA MODEL

HEMY'S
PIANOFORTE TUTOR

METZLER & CO

CPSIA information can be obtained at www.ICGtesting.com
Printed in the USA
BVOW01s1021060115

382139BV00018B/299/P